PRAISE FOR *BAGGY RED PANTS AND OTHER STORIES*:

"*Baggy Red Pants and Other Stories* brings Stephen's psyche-folk-music mindset onto the page with stories that transport me across wide-open roads, from Gallup, NM to Canadian provinces, to hippie communes, to movie sets, to warehouse loading docks, to a music festival on Mars. We meet pig farmers, trash-talking dock workers, a crazed shooter, a Canadian Mountie, hippie girlfriends, an indie cult film director, and winos straight out of a John Steinbeck novel. The narrative gets as close as a switch-blade-to-the-neck and so far away that everything appears miniature, insignificant, unimportant—so why take ourselves so seriously? Why stress over the late bus? Let's hitch a ride, take a trip with this hitchhiker and see where we go. After all, he's wearing those far out baggy red pants!"

—CHRISTOPHER SHOTOLA-HARDT, artist

* # *

"I just read Stephen Cohen's charming book. He provides the lucky reader with glimpses into his life by writing scintillating vignettes and sharing his art pieces, poems and lyrics. His is a rare kind of creativity, one that uses everything at his disposal to make something novel and enchanting. This book is proof of his creative genius."

—BONNIE BOSTROM, author of *Born Crazy* and others

* # *

"To read *Baggy Red Pants,* is to be drawn into the magical world of Stephen Cohen, a world of eternal youth and innocence, crazy off-kilter rhythms, and infectious motifs. His writing, like his music, follows a syncopated beat with a logic of the heart. In his life of hippie hijinx, we glimpse a Tibetan sand painting, that dazzles with its colors and contours then is swept away and seen no more. Like a pair of magical baggy red trousers that dance across the landscape, then disappear into smoke and flames."

—RICH HINRICHSEN, musician and mathematician

* # *

"3 Hand Stephen writes in the way he sings. He takes us on a gentle journey that lets us see the unexpected in everyday moments. A path that leaves us with the feeling that what seems to be normal could be magical if we open our eyes and see with our heart."

—EFRAIN ROZAS, musical artist

* # *

Thomas liked to sing his secret songs.
And if the world is not right with Thomas, then something must be wrong.
—from *Thomas* by Stephen Cohen

"Stephen Cohen's world is keenly observed and deeply felt. He shares all of it, in many media, with all of us. Stephen's deceptively simple poetry can pack an emotional punch. His music resonates on many levels—charming and playful, as are his hand-crafted jewelry, art and instruments, yet often poignant and bittersweet. His unique work is heartfelt, haunting and lovely."

—AMY COHEN, artist

* # *

"The stories, visual art, and songs in this book are magical and ominous portraits of humans in our times. Like T.C. Boyle or Neil Gaiman, Stephen creates an art stew that tastes innocent, earthy, playful and is tinged with pain. You will be full after reading, and will come back for more."

—KATE DAVIS, writer and social worker

PRAISE FOR STEPHEN COHEN'S WORK:

"Stephen Cohen has a knack for mixing music and art. He makes jewelry out of guitar strings and whimsical pins that look like instruments. His nearly 6-foot-tall sculpture that looks like a robot created out of spare parts from around the home is a perfect blend of art and music, a made-up instrument with a playable belly and face, and brass cymbals for hands."

—HEATHER RAYHORN, *Statesman Journal* (Salem, Oregon)

* # *

"Stephen Cohen has lived in a treehouse in the mountains, in geodesic domes and makeshift shacks in several communes, and is a performing, recording and visual artist using voice, cigar box guitars, acoustic guitar and a one-of-a-kind miniature guitar in one-of-a-kind performances. His song *Miniature Planet*, a musical contemplation like no other, is so very relevant in these fractured times."

—BRIAN CUTEAN, *SE Examiner*

BAGGY RED PANTS AND OTHER STORIES

Short Stories, Poems, Lyrics and Visual Art

BAGGY RED PANTS and OTHER STORIES

SHORT STORIES, POEMS, LYRICS AND VISUAL ART

by

3 HAND STEPHEN

Baggy Red Pants and Other Stories
Short Stories, Poems, Lyrics and Visual Art
by 3 Hand Stephen

Printed in the United States of America

First Edition: August 3, 2021
ISBN 978-1-946970-10-7
Library of Congress Control Number: 2021913616

Published by

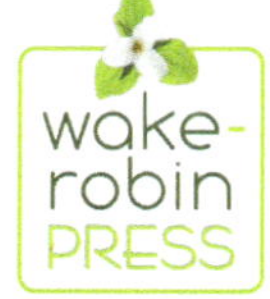

Wake-Robin Press
An imprint of redbat books
La Grande, OR 97850
www.wakerobinpress.com

Text set in Alegreya and ElliotSix

Title Art Painted by
3 Hand Stephen
www.3handstephen.com

Cover Design & Book Layout by
redbat design | www.redbatdesign.com

TABLE OF CONTENTS

I dedicate this book to all my family, friends, and musical and artistic colleagues.
You have been there for me through so much. Thank you!

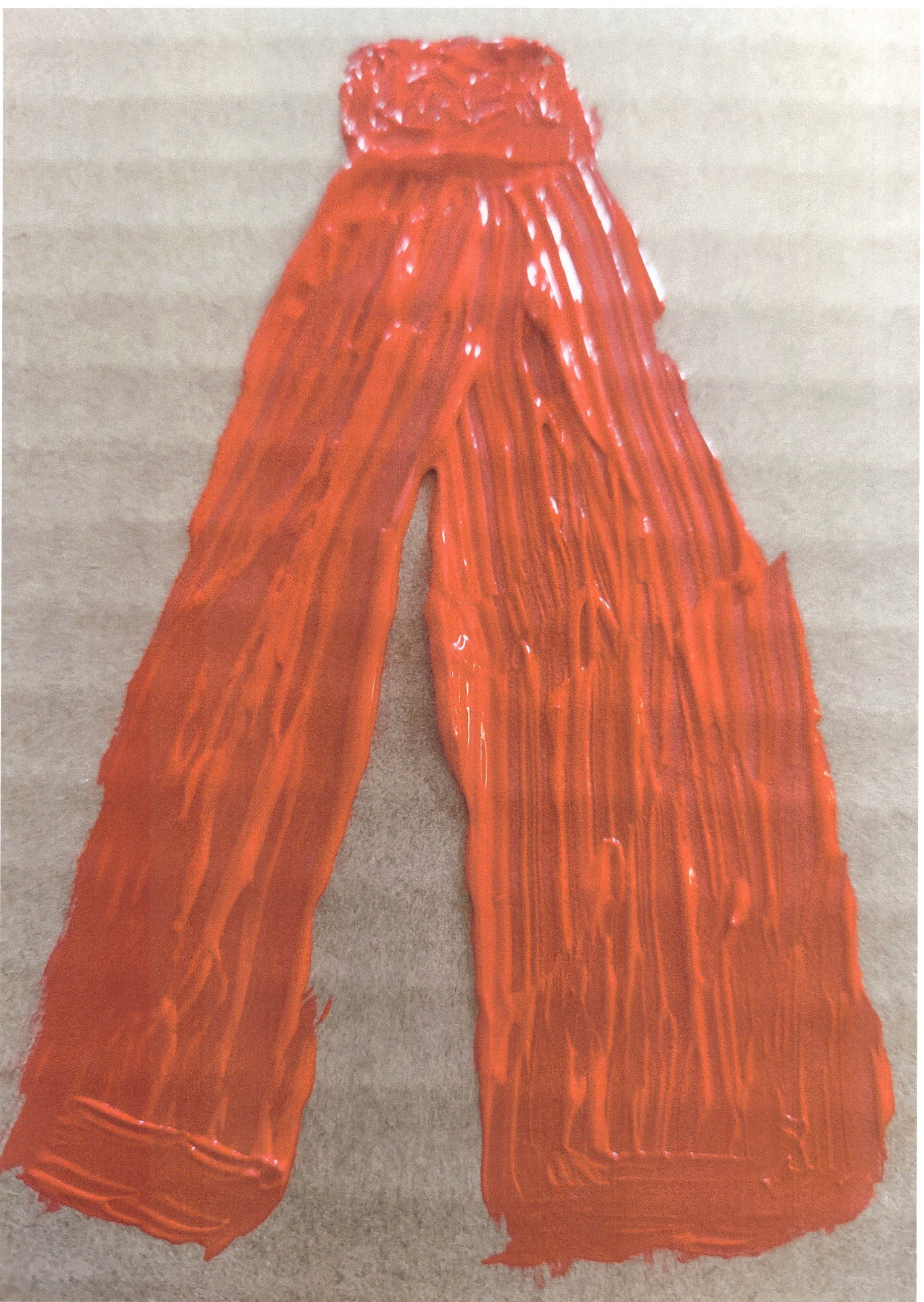

BAGGY RED PANTS

We arrived in Santa Fe in those hitchhiking days.
I was wearing baggy red pants that my girlfriend had made
Baggy, baggy, homemade baggy, baggy, baggy, baggy red pants
I needed some guitar strings, so I found the local music store
I was wearing those baggy red pants as I walked out the door
Into the plaza where a tall bespectacled Englishman approached by chance
He said, "I'm producing a movie; would you like to be in it? Meet me tomorrow
    and wear those red pants"
Baggy, baggy, homemade baggy, baggy, baggy, baggy red pants
We slept in an alley that night. In the morning we met the cast and crew
    at a plaza hotel
We boarded a charter bus to go film a rock musical
    based on Shakespeare's Othello.
The producer was impresario Jack Good. The movie was called "Catch My Soul."
The set was a fake hippie commune in the desert hills, 10 miles up the road
Baggy, baggy, homemade baggy, baggy, baggy, baggy red pants
I worked as an extra in that movie, every day for 2 months I wore those red pants
One night they brought in 100 local hipsters for a party scene that turned into
    a stoned, chaotic dance
Baggy, baggy, homemade baggy, baggy, baggy, baggy red pants
"Catch My Soul" opened in New York City, got some bad reviews
    and quickly disappeared
It stayed lost for 42 years but then reappeared
I did other work for Jack Good, a good guy, who died last year
As for the pants, we threw them in the fire and watched the ashes float
    into the mountain air
Baggy, baggy, homemade baggy, baggy, baggy, baggy red pants

A HITCHHIKER'S TALE

A Volkswagen Bus full of freaks was definitely the best thing for a young hitchhiker to see coming his way in the summer of '72. A pickup with an older couple of pig farmers in Colorado could also be good. Such a couple picked me up, took me to their farm, introduced me to their pigs, cooked me dinner, and put me up for the night. The only thing they asked in exchange was conversation, so they could hear "what the young people these days are thinking."

A huge long-haul truck with a lone driver could also be promising. Such a driver could take you a long way, maybe even to New Orleans and Mardi Gras, as that trucker who picked me up in Texas did. I don't know why he let the Grand Funk Railroad tape on his eight-track play over and over again for hours, coming around again and again to the song "I'm Getting Closer to My Home." Maybe it had something to do with the endless supply of marijuana in his curtained cab.

But there I was, standing on an Arizona highway with my guitar, backpack, and sleeping bag, and a Volkswagen Bus full of freaks sure looked good. And it figured because, on the road, good would often follow bad. Good followed bad on the coast highway near Malibu.

A middle-aged, casually-dressed man picked me up in his camper and, after a few miles of silence, he pulled into a cutaway by the beach. He said we would be taking a break, then got out, took out a gun, and started shooting indiscriminately into the twilight air. There was movement among the scattered groups of people on the beach. A sandy-haired young man approached me and said, "Let's get out of here!" I quickly joined a group of surfers in a funky van, speeding away from the mystery shooter, winding through the coastal night until we arrived at a secluded cove. I joined my new friends in a wonderful cookout by a campfire, then slept on the beach to the sound of the waves crashing on the shore.

Good followed bad and a crazy game of tag through the Canadian plains on a northern hitchhiking trip with a girlfriend. A souped-up sedan driven by a dark-haired, stone-eyed man swerved right at us in an obvious attempt to either hit or scare us. Scare us it did and, while we were wondering if he was coming back for more, a [Royal] Canadian Mounted Police car approached.

The officer didn't check our I.D. or kick us off the highway as his United States counterparts would often do. He merely offered us a ride and gave us smooth, friendly passage to the next province.

Things turned bad again in that next province, as a cloud of black flies filled the sky and descended upon us. Cars drove by as if we were invisible. Just when we thought we would be eaten alive by the tiny biting insects, the sweetest couple pulled up in a station wagon and offered us a night's lodging in exchange for a song on my guitar. Safe inside a cozy house somewhere in the middle of Canada, I played the sweetest song I could for that couple and their wide-eyed baby. Later on down the road we ran out of money. We were miles away from our destination, tired and hungry, and things looked bad. Suddenly a man on a motorcycle appeared as if in a vision. He was wearing a white jump suit with red trim and a matching helmet. He stopped and handed us each a twenty-dollar bill, then rode off into the hills.

And now good and bad were at it again, chasing each other down the desert highway. I had slept in the brush overlooking a deep quarry outside of Gallup, New Mexico. I awoke and headed into town, where I was greeted by a trio of winos. They wanted to know my nationality ("American, man") and invited me to stop and drink wine with them. The oldest, toughest looking one handed me his bottle but it accidentally slipped out of my hands and fell to the sidewalk. I suddenly felt the flash of a switchblade at my neck. I talked fast, apologizing profusely, and the switchblade went back into its holder. We shook hands and I took my leave.

I had seen enough of Gallup and caught the next available ride out, in an old Dodge Dart with an Ohio license plate. Three men in their early twenties, friends from childhood, were on a cross-country adventure. Good-natured joking mixed with stories of the road, as we sped out of New Mexico into Arizona. But then flashing lights were seen behind us: those Ohio plates had expired dates, and a patrolman had noticed. He instructed us to follow him to the courthouse in the next town. It was a small-town courthouse like in the movies, an old square brick building with an old square-jawed judge inside. The judge levied an outrageous fine. One of the travelers paid it, but swore in anger as he started to walk out the building. A policeman rushed out of an office door and said, "That's contempt of court!" The young man was given a choice of either an even more outrageous bail (more than any of us had) or a night in jail. At this point there was nothing I could do, so I thanked them for the ride and left the courthouse as they discussed what friends or relatives they might call to wire them the money. I stood on the main street and tried to hitchhike out, but a policeman pulled up to tell me that hitchhiking was illegal within the city limits. With guitar in hand, backpack and sleeping bag on my back, I walked for an hour, as far away as I could. And that is how I ended up on that desert highway at sunset in the summer of '72, with a Volkswagen Bus full of freaks heading my way.

"Come on in, we're going to the Strawberry Canyon Hot Springs. Do you want to come with us?" That sounded good to me. There were eight people in the bus, four of them friends from Minnesota and four of them assorted hitchhikers. We went off the main highway, wound through canyons and piñon pine-spotted hills, and arrived at the hot springs in the dark of night. There was a skinny river with a sandy, level area on one side and a rocky cliff on the other. Ten feet up the cliff was a ledge with two circular hot spring pools. Farther along the ledge were the cracked pink cement ruins of a long-abandoned health resort. I climbed up to the ledge and took out my guitar. I touched my fingers to the steel strings and a freckle-faced, red-haired woman named Ginger (one of the Minnesota contingent) took out an old guitar. One of those special jams that can only happen on the road commenced. We played like we had been playing together for years. A skinny, energetic teenager put together a makeshift drum set out of guitar cases, sticks, and rocks, and played along in perfect rhythm. Two women started dancing on the ledge's edge, their naked bodies silhouetted by the stars. Later, we let the last notes trail off into the canyon, put our instruments away, and lay in the hot pools for a while. I then jumped into the river below. The night desert air dried my hair as I lay on my sleeping bag in the sand by the river and drifted off to sleep under a canopy of stars.

* # *

we are inside
looking out
and outside
looking in
it feels like the world
is closed until further notice

but the trees are talking
the birds are singing
the stars are shining

life is open all around us

from me

to you

tHE CLOSING LISt

turn the signs, close the blinds, lock the door
count the till, clean the grill, sweep and mop the floor
put all the receipts in a drawer
put the dry goods in a bin, put the wet goods in the walk-ins
clean the ovens and the countertops and the silver and the pans and pots
turn off the dishwashing machine after you get everything restaurant clean
prepare a statement for the bank, put the money in the safe
say goodnight to the help, thank you, you don't need their help anymore
take off your restaurant clothes, move across the restaurant floor
there's no restaurant here anymore
count the till, clean the grill, sweep and mop the floor
change the signs, shut the blinds, put a padlock on the door
there's no restaurant here anymore, anymore, anymore

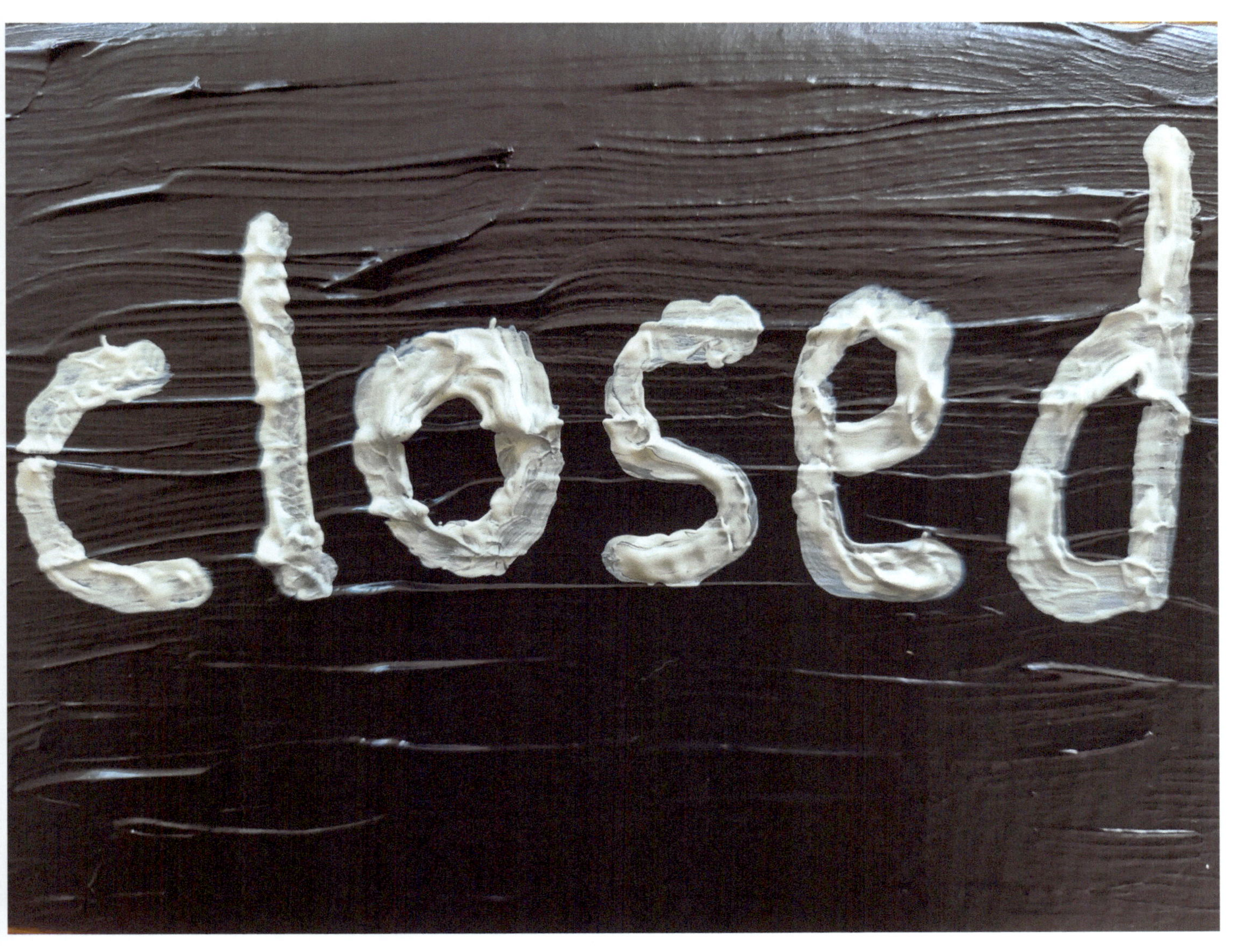
closed

THOMAS

There was a little boy named Thomas. He was a little bit shy.
He would not play with the other kids. He would not look you in the eye.
He just recited numbers, just as far as he could go.
Thomas liked to stage his secret shows.
The first time I saw Thomas, it was in a special school.
I took him to the music room. He sat down on a stool.
He yelled monster at the piano. I yelled danger at the drums.
Thomas liked to sing his secret songs.
There was a little boy named Thomas. He was a little bit strange.
He liked to spin in circles and he smiled as he sang.
He really was intelligent. People called him slow.
Thomas liked to stage his special shows.
The last time I saw Thomas, he was crying in a yard.
A friend of his was leaving and he always took things hard.
I yelled danger at the piano. He yelled monster at the drums.
Thomas liked to sing his secret songs.
And if the world is not right with Thomas, then something must be wrong.

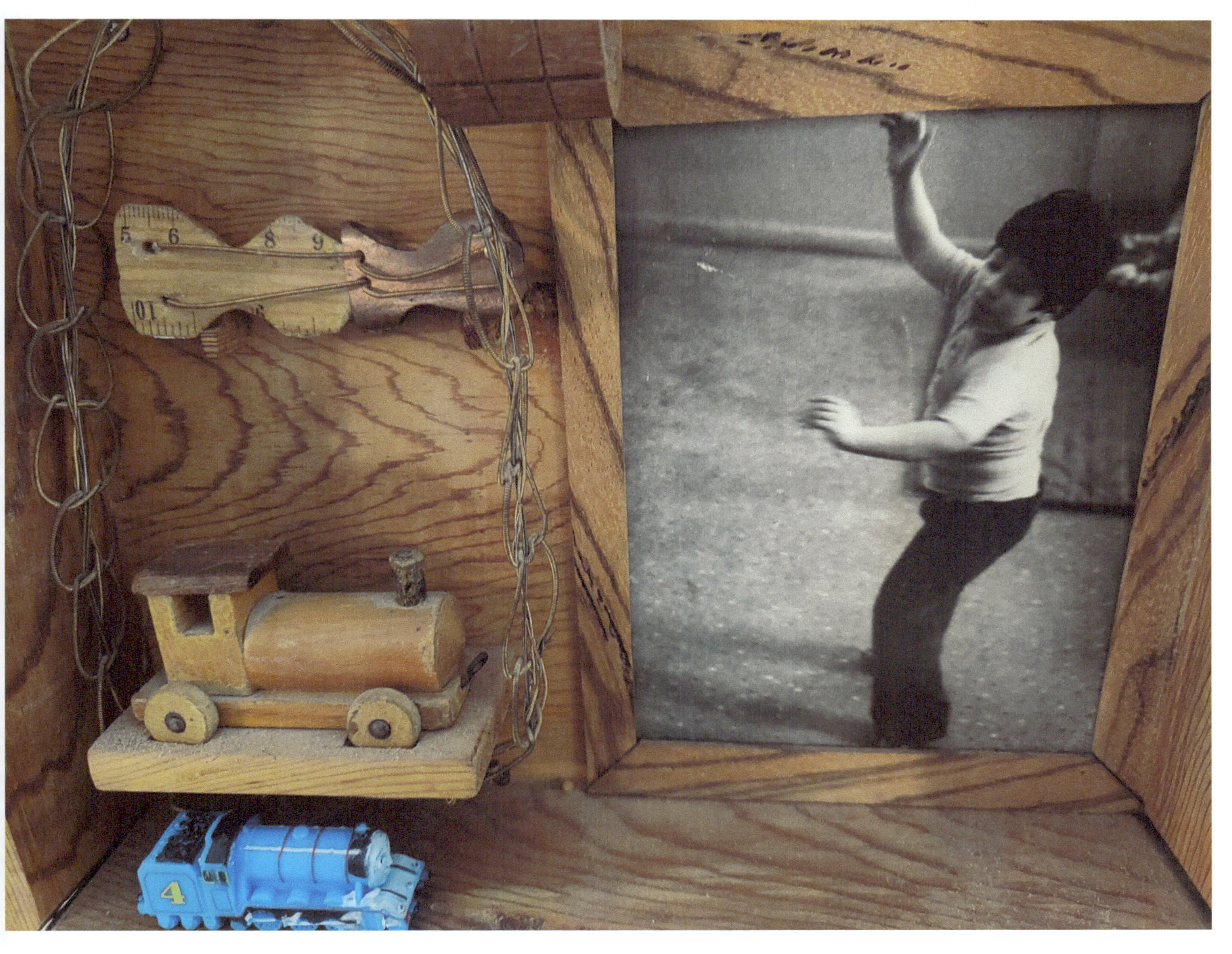

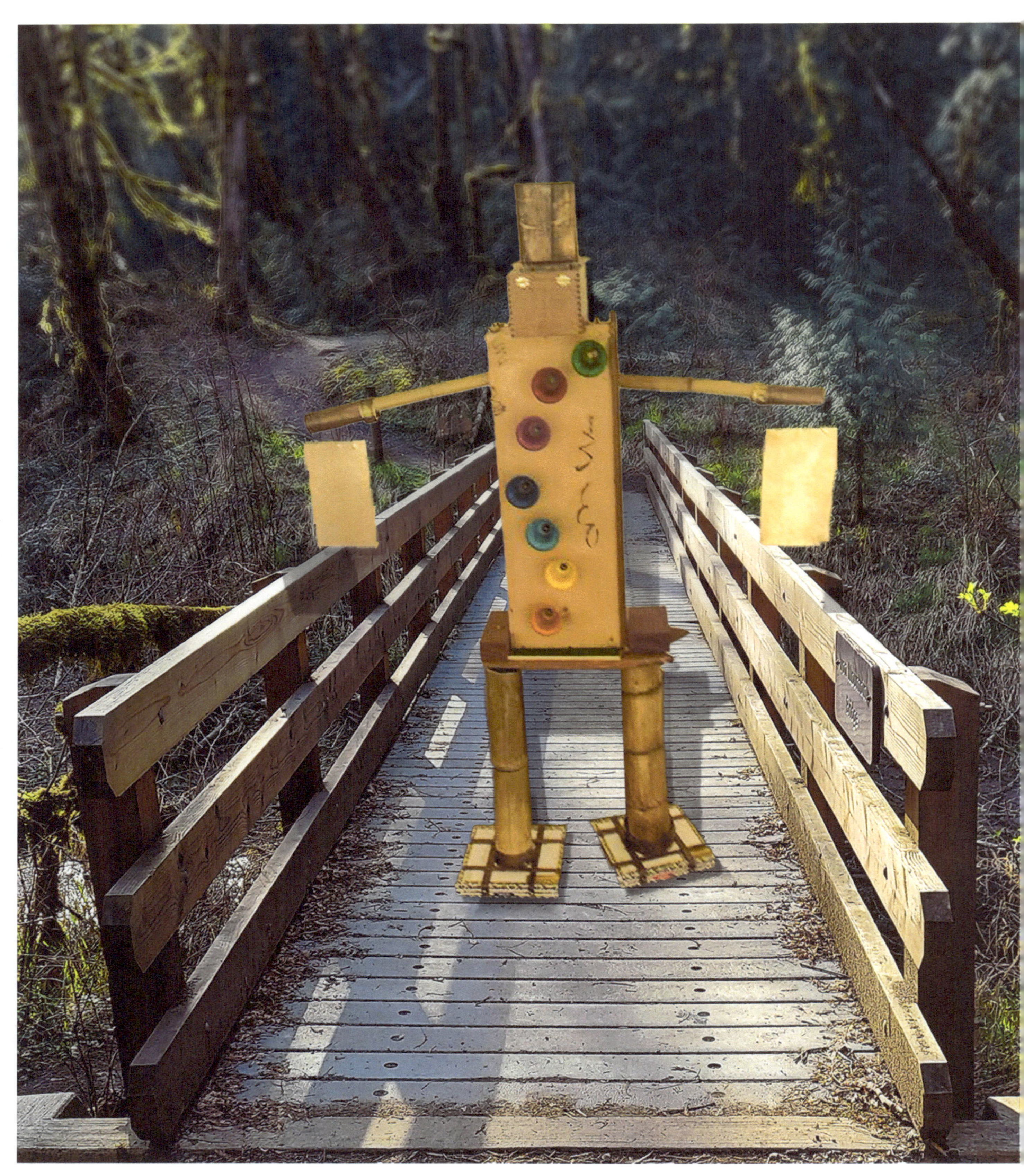

MR. BELLS

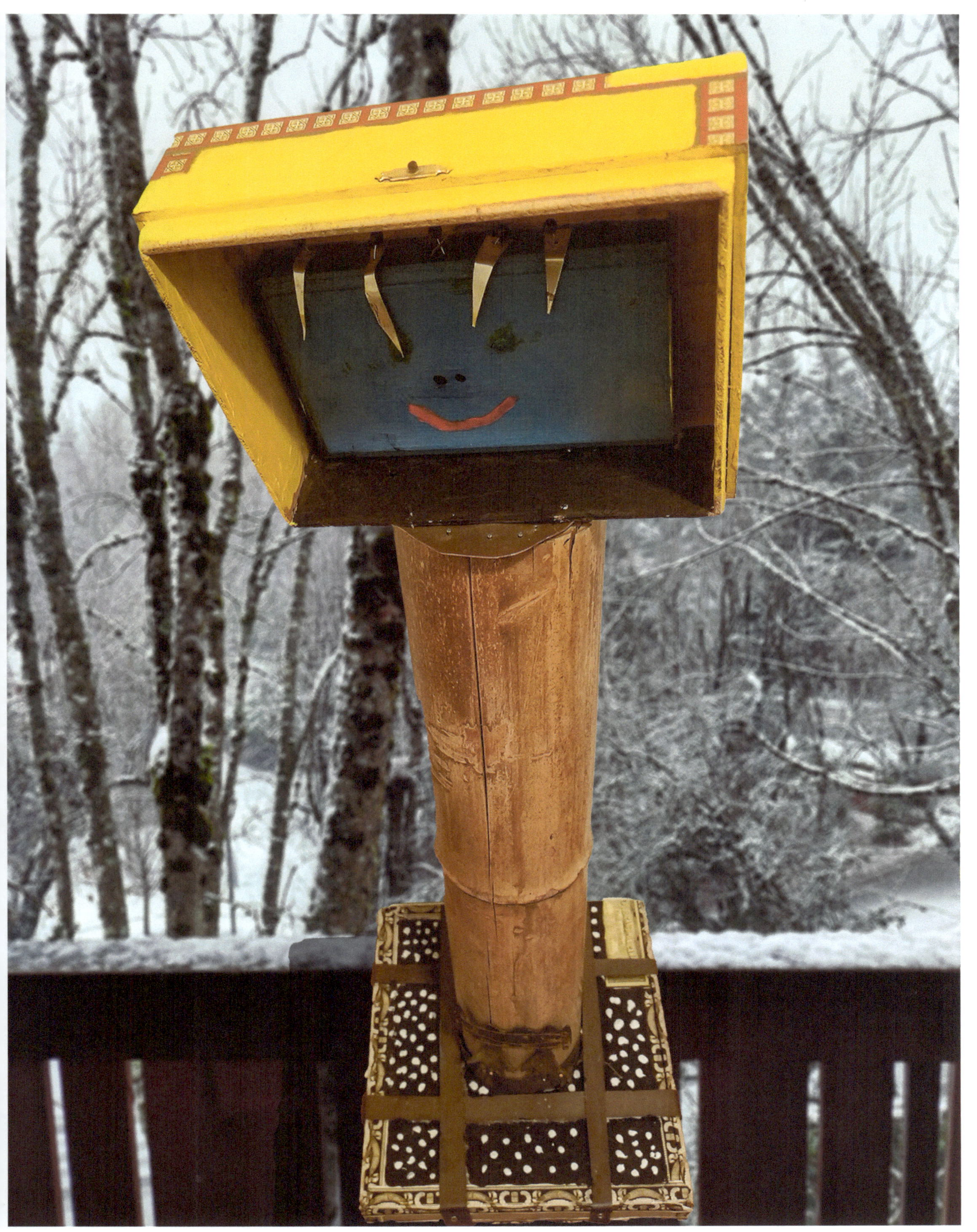

MS. GREETER

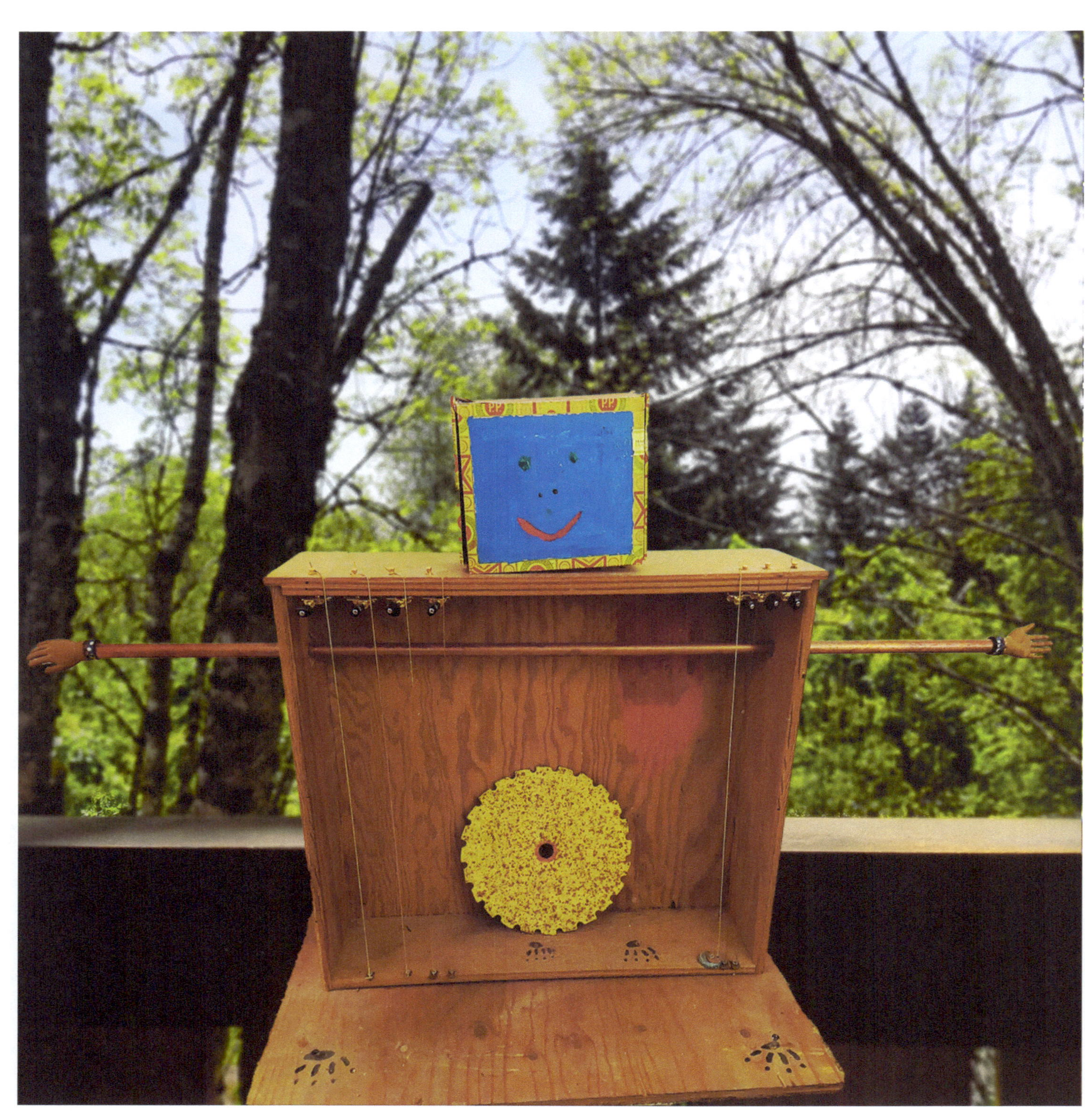

SISTER 7 STRINGS

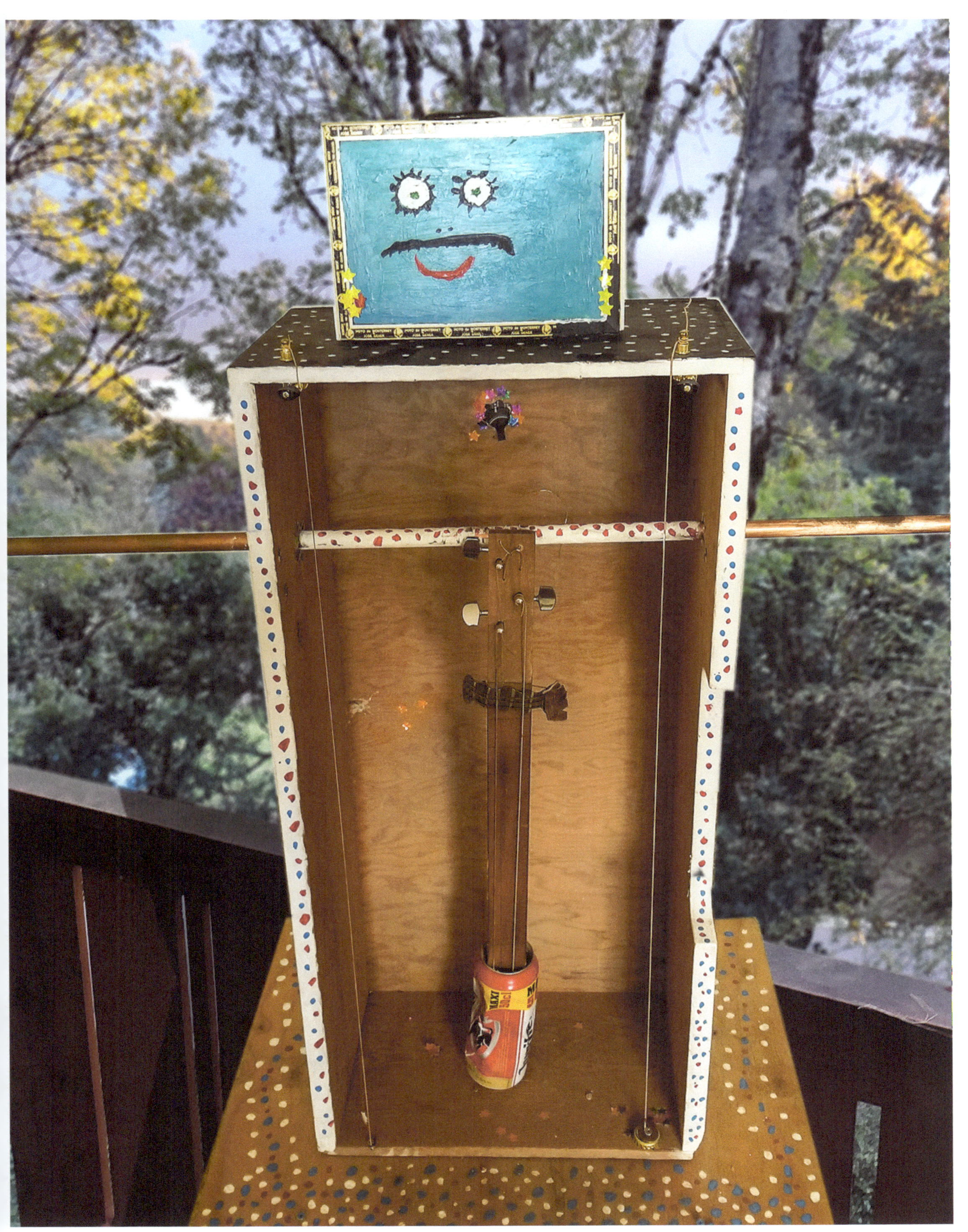

BROTHER STEPHEN

KING OF THE 1-STRING THINGS

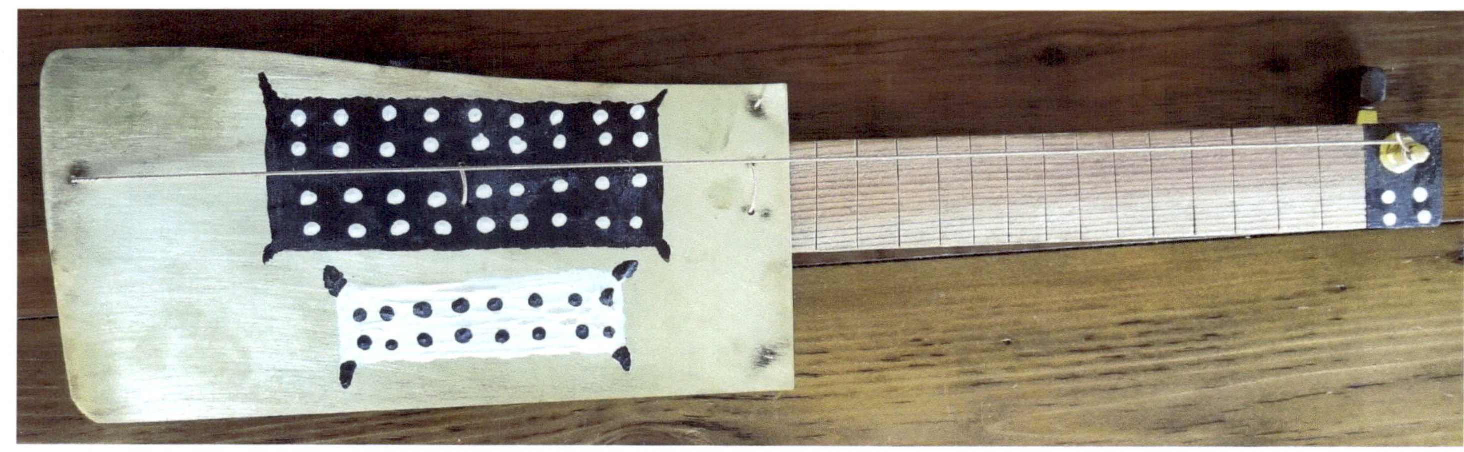

I'm the King, I'm the King, I'm the King of the 1-String Things
I can do the 1-string thing
I can make the 1-String Things sing

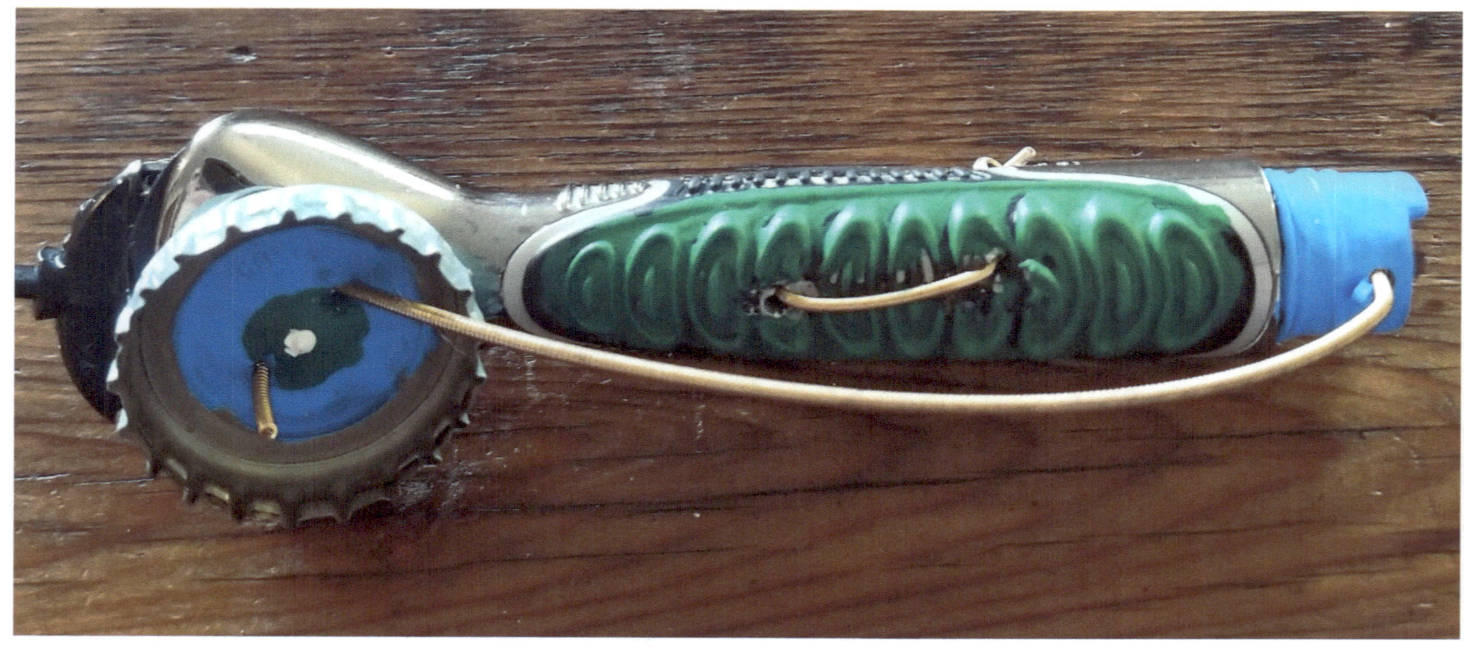

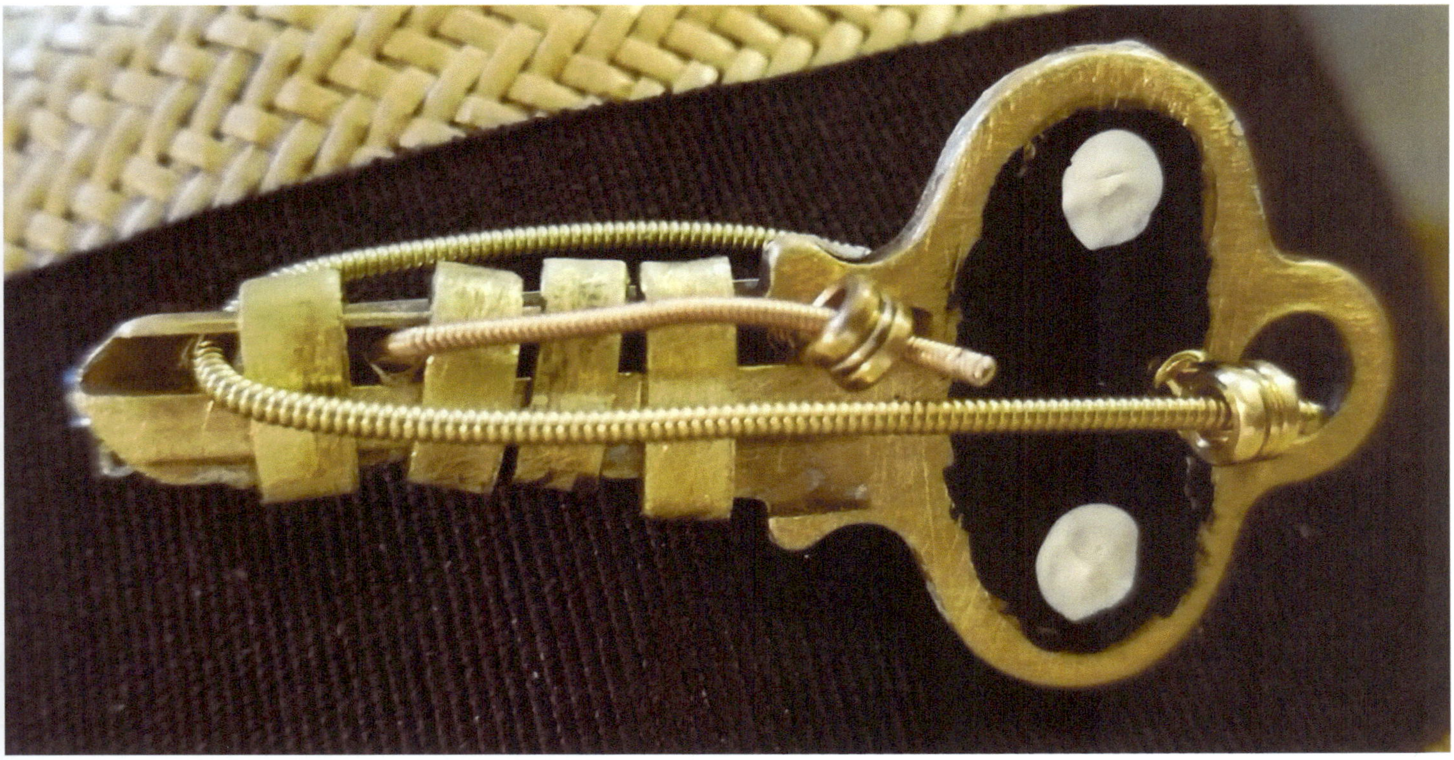

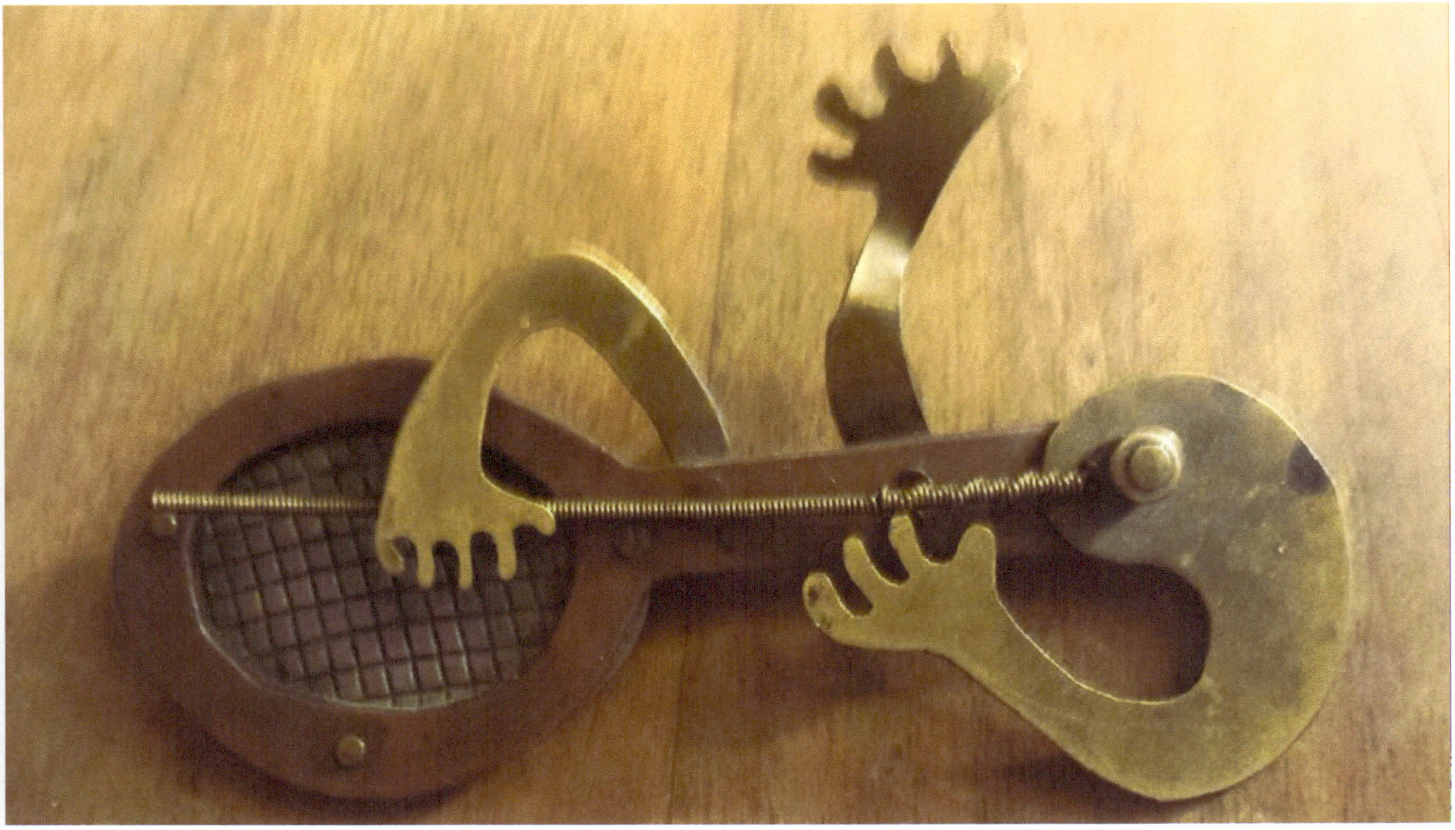

LET'S ALL ROOT FOR THE HOME TEAM

let's all root for the home team, it's the only team we know, go, home team, go
let's all root for the home team, we've got to win this game
we can't afford another season down the drain
players run the hardwood floor as quick as they can
to ten thousand voices, noises, the band
cheerleaders leap, show a silly smile to the faithful fans who stand in the aisles
the coach paces down the sidelines like a caged beast
sweat is falling, he is calling, he cannot stand defeat
outside the ticket-taker looks into the rain
we've got to win this game
let's all root for the home team, it's the only team we like, fight, home team, fight
let's all root for the home team, we've got to win this game
we can't afford another season down the drain
the street is full of people who are shaking their heads
the locker room is quite like a knife
I guess you know the news, the home team is not supposed to lose
let's all root for the home team, it's the only team we see, victory,
    home team, victory
let's all root for the home team, we've got to win this game
we can't afford another season down the drain

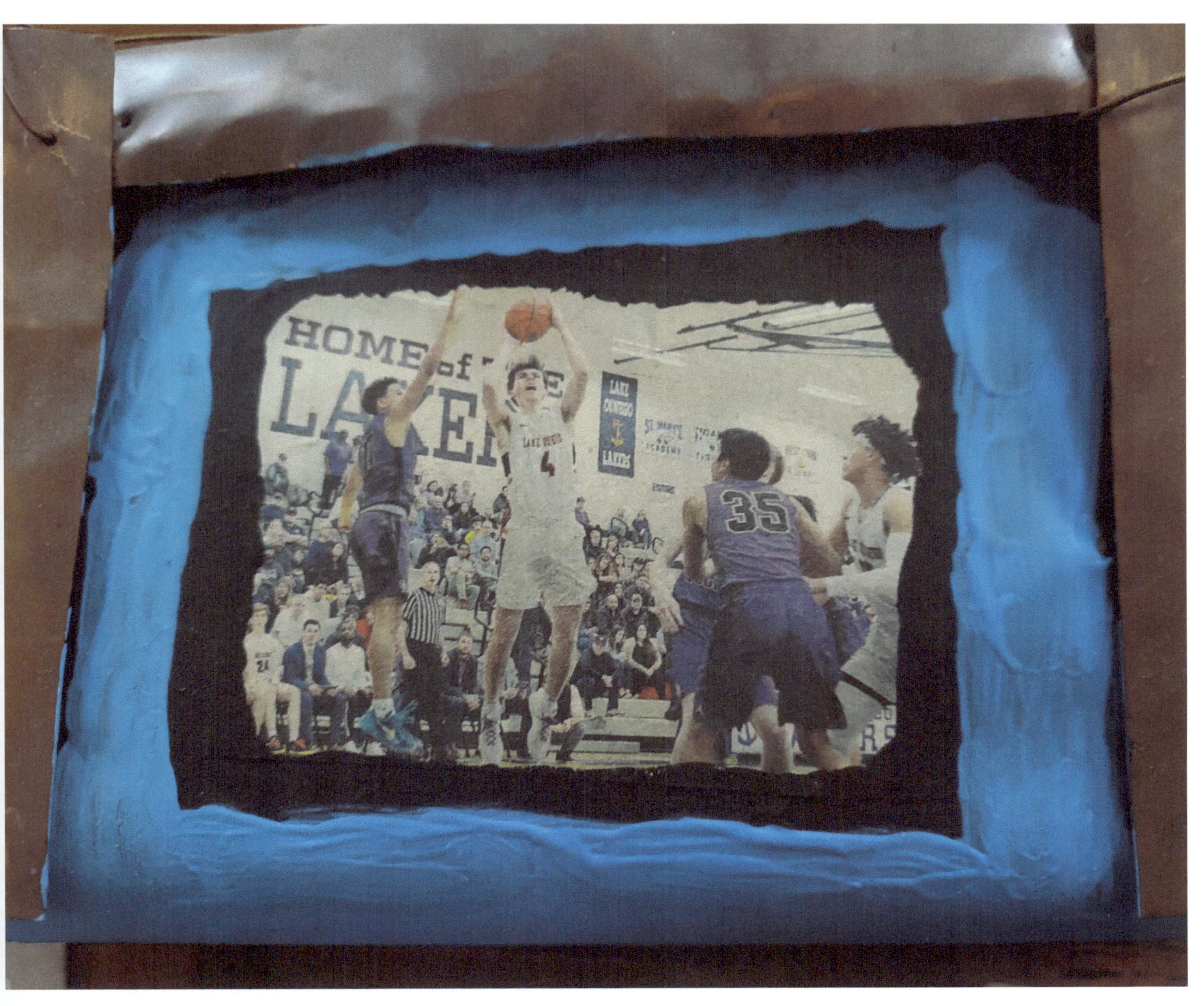
HOME
LAKE OSWEGO
LAKERS

THE BARKING DOG AT DUCK DELIVERY

"Get me 2 #90 spuds, 1 medium tomato, 2 each oregano, 3 each tarragon," a man wearing a Duck Delivery cap barked from behind a wooden podium. "Get me 1 dozen lettuce, 2 dozen romaine, 10 lbs. spin clean, 5 each eggplant." He was one of three checkers on the dock. Each stood behind a podium with delivery printouts in hand. A line of loaders with empty hand trucks would approach, listen to the checker's request, go into the large refrigerated rooms to get the produce, pile the boxes on the hand truck, return to the dock to recite back to the checker, "1 medium tomato, 2 #90 spuds, 2 each oregano, 3 each tarragon," then load the boxes into a designated truck on the dock.

All through the long night there was the constant sound of the loaders and checkers filling orders and of trucks pulling in and out of the dock. In a small office in a small corner overlooking it all you could hear the hum of a fax machine spitting out new orders and the intermittent ring of the office phone. Many of the loaders were from Mexico, and some sang popular Mexican songs as they moved through three large refrigerated rooms in search of the requested fruits and vegetables. And there was the sound of the lift operator Paulo driving a forklift around restocking supplies and moving boxes here and there while keeping up a running commentary of good-natured insults directed at the loaders. Paulo, a heavy-set man himself, especially liked to call John, one of the bigger loaders, "Keiko," in honor of the celebrity whale. John would just answer, "Shut your fucking trap, Paulo!"

At one podium stood Jose the checker, patiently giving out instructions. At another stood the bearded chain-smoking checker David. But always standing at the same podium to the right, rooted behind it like a small thick tree, always wearing black-rimmed glasses, a Duck Delivery cap, blue jeans, black shoes, and a shiny company jacket, was the legendary Bob, better known to the loaders and the drivers as the Barking Dog. "#90 spuds, not #80, go back and get it right! Those are large tomatoes, I said medium! What took you so long, did you grow the lettuce yourself?

Most of Bob's wrath was directed at new people at Duck Delivery. He was a barking dog in that way, barking mostly to strangers in his territory. He was the obstacle everyone had to pass through to enter the domain of Duck Delivery. It was sad—kind of touching—

to see new people struggle so hard to get it right, to try to remember what the checker said, then to wander lost in the cold warehouse looking for vegetables they never heard of like spin clean (slang for washed spinach) or mescaline or portabella. And they received no sympathy at all from the Barking Dog. "I said tarragon. Don't you know what that is? Get me some now!" The more confused and frazzled they became, the worse it would get. "Two each oregano, not two dozen! Put the extras back! I don't believe it! You put it in a box like that! And you want to be a driver? Why are you guys taking so long putting those boxes in that truck? Are you having a circle jerk? I need these orders sometime today!"

An intense, thin, blond, mustached man named Curtis sat in a small crowded office overlooking the dock. As each truck was loaded the checker would bring a printout to the office and receive the next truck's printout from Curtis, who would put the filled printouts in metal binders on a shelf outside the office window for the drivers, who would arrive to work between two and four in the morning. The drivers would check their printouts, then join the parade of loaders to look for any unchecked items or to help on other orders until their own trucks were cleared to go. Curtis also spent his time in the office scheduling drivers, taking additional orders on the phone or fax machine, scrambling on the phone to find last minute sources when produce supplies were running low, giving drivers directions on the large map, or meeting with Lawrence, the company manager.

Lawrence was a small, fifty-year-old man with dark black hair, an olive complexion, and small, constantly moving brown eyes. He occasionally showed up on the dock to observe the proceedings, exchange greetings with the checkers, loaders, and drivers, and visit Curtis in his little office. But most of the time Lawrence was in his own little office upstairs on the other side of the building. One winter morning a man named Craig walked into Lawrence's little office for a job interview. Craig was in his young thirties, newly arrived from Michigan, with a face that looked tough and sensitive, sad and happy, all at the same time. Lawrence shook Craig's hand then started talking. "We need new drivers now. Our business is growing quickly. We are getting new accounts every week. We used to supply produce to many of the supermarkets in town, but now the big chains have their own warehouses, trucks, and drivers. But restaurants, specialty markets, delicatessens, schools, hospitals, and hotels all want our business and we have to work hard to keep up. We are looking to hire four or five new drivers in the next few months. I see on your application that you've worked as a driver and had some restaurant experience."

"Yes," Craig answered. "I always thought produce drivers had it pretty good, driving around with fruits and vegetables all day, and being home every night."

"Well, sometimes it can be okay," Lawrence replied, "but it is very fast-paced, there is some lifting involved, and most shifts begin between two and four in the morning. Do you think you can handle it?"

"I've handled a lot in my life," Craig quietly answered. "I can handle it."

"Well, like I say, we need new drivers now," as his eyes darted up and down from the application to Craig.

"I've got a list of references." Craig offered.

Lawrence shook his head dismissively. "I don't put any stock in references. I can tell you are a good person by talking with you. I know people. The job is yours if you want it. The first week, as all new drivers do, you will work nights loading trucks so you can learn the product, then after that we'll get you a route. When can you start?"

The first sound Craig heard as he walked across the dock was the Barking Dog's loud voice. "Get me 1 dozen green leaf, 1 dozen red-leaf, 1 each red cabbage, 2 each green cabbage." It was nine o'clock on a Sunday night and Craig reported to Curtis' office to start his training week as a loader.

"It's a memory thing," Curtis told Craig as they looked out into the circus on the dock. "We'll start you out with a few items at a time, then build to four or more items. After a week you should be familiar with the product and I'll send you out to learn with a few of my best drivers for a few days, then I'll get you a route of your own. Get one of those extra hand trucks and Bob will get you started."

Craig fell into the line of loaders and the long night began. He wandered through the refrigerated rooms searching for fruits and vegetables, piled up boxes in his hand truck, called back his filled orders to the checker and put the boxes in the trucks, over and over again. He received the standard insults from the Barking Dog, but Craig figured it would take a lot more than a big-mouthed barking bully to drive him from this job. He tried ignoring the Barking Dog, then he tried yelling back at him, "How do you expect me to find Shiitake mushrooms when there are none back there?" Humor seemed to work best. "No, I wasn't growing the lettuce, I was out in the fields picking it. I put it in a box like that because I'm new and don't know what the hell I'm doing." He discovered that Paulo the fork-lift driver knew where everything was and was happy to share that information. Craig knew he could do this job okay.

Others did not fare so well. There was another new driver in training, a serious-looking guy with short hair and wire-rimmed glasses, who Craig heard hissing at the Barking Dog. "If you yell at me one more time, I'm leaving."

The Barking Dog said nothing, and seemed extra careful not to demean the guy in any way for about an hour or two, until finally he couldn't control himself anymore and barked at him for mixing up kale with fennel.

"That's it!" the serious-looking guy said as he threw his hand truck down and walked off the dock, disappearing into the darkness.

That incident became the talk of the dock among the workers. One thought the Barking Dog was too hard on people and needed to loosen up. One new worker said, "You know, if I was starting a business, I would hire Bob the Barking Dog in a heartbeat to help run it. He would get things done right."

As they worked deep into the night Craig noticed that his jacket, his hands, and his fingernails were all stained with vegetables and dirt. He felt the cold air in the refrigerated rooms through his body, through his whole self. He felt he had joined a new subterranean race that lived in refrigerated rooms. The drivers started to arrive, bringing fresh energy and purpose to the dock. They looked confident and competent. Even the Barking Dog treated them with respect. Lawrence was out on the dock, shaking hands and smiling like a politician on the stump. He saw Craig and asked him how it was going. "Good," Craig replied, and continued working.

After a while Craig could see a hint of morning light in the dark sky. Most of the trucks were loaded and gone. "Break time!" the Barking Dog announced, and the loaders and a few remaining drivers spread about the dock, sitting on boxes and pallets. Craig sat on a box of jumbo yellow onions near Curtis' little office and noticed that Curtis and Lawrence were in there with a tired, scraggly haired driver. Lawrence was not smiling anymore. "All we're saying is that is time for you to pick up the pace. Customers are complaining about getting their orders late."

"I'm working as hard as I can," the driver replied. Maybe you need to adjust the route."

Curtis fixed his intense stare on the man. "Joe didn't seem have any trouble when he had your route."

"That's because Joe drives like a maniac and doesn't take his lunch break," the driver answered. "You do want us to drive safely, don't you?"

"Look," Lawrence said. "We're happy with the effort you've been putting forth. We just want you to pick up the pace a little bit. And we appreciate that your drug tests have been clean since that problem last year."

Curtis shuffled some schedules around his desk and looked down as he said, "Maybe I made a mistake putting you on this route. I could switch you to a shorter route and that might work."

"Oh no, don't cut my hours again. You know my money situation is not good."

As words continued to float out of the little office, the sky outside turned red and blue. Two female dispatchers, one in a green dress and one in tight jeans, heels, and a pink sweater, arrived and walked across the dock to the little office, moving in unison with the sound of their high voices rising to the roof of the dock like birdsong. A salesman in a dark suit sauntered by, staring at the dispatchers' behinds. Paulo started moving boxes around again with his forklift, and yelled to his favorite loader, "Hey Keiko, go back to the ocean!"

"Shut your fucking trap, Paulo," John answered.

One of the loaders started singing in Spanish. The Barking Dog barked, "Break is over. Let's get this place cleaned up so we can get out of here. You over there, get up! Do you need a special invitation?"

Craig looked out towards the street as he helped clean up the dock. The shining sun was peeking through tall city buildings in the distance.

Craig got his own route after a few weeks and settled into the daily routine of delivering produce to local businesses. There was a lot to like about driving at sunrise in the company of fruits and vegetables but it didn't really pay that well, so after six months he left Duck Delivery for a new job with better pay and benefits. But his time at Duck Delivery left a lasting impression and in the future he would go out to eat at the best restaurants he had discovered on his route, like one restaurant in which Craig had noticed the care the chef had shown while personally checking each order. One day after breakfast downtown, Craig walked out into the street and saw Carlos, a Duck Delivery driver who had started working there the week that Craig had left. Carlos told him the latest news from Duck Delivery. Bob the Barking Dog had gone back to his previous career as a long-haul trucker, and was gone, gone, gone, but not forgotten.

Craig could still hear the Barking Dog in his dreams: "Get me 1 red delicious, 1 green delicious, 1 jumbo onions, 1 each oregano, 1 each cilantro."

* # *

YOUR BUS IS LATE

There are reasons why your bus could be late.
ignition, transmission, driver decision, vehicle collision, traffic stopped,
    traffic cop, detour, wet floor, stuck door, stray pup, bridge up, construction,
    obstruction, long wait,
your bus is late
baggage roller, baby stroller, fare inspection, accident in intersection,
    traffic congestion, fire truck, garbage truck, truck stuck, ramp stuck,
    tow truck, bad luck, long wait,
your bus is late
crossing kids, icy skids, driver out of chair, police in riot gear, march for peace,
    crossing geese, ducks in road, dogs in road, horse in road, cow in road,
    plow in road, snow on ground, passenger down, bikes in lane, freezing rain,
    passing train, crossing gate, twist of fate,
long wait
your bus is late

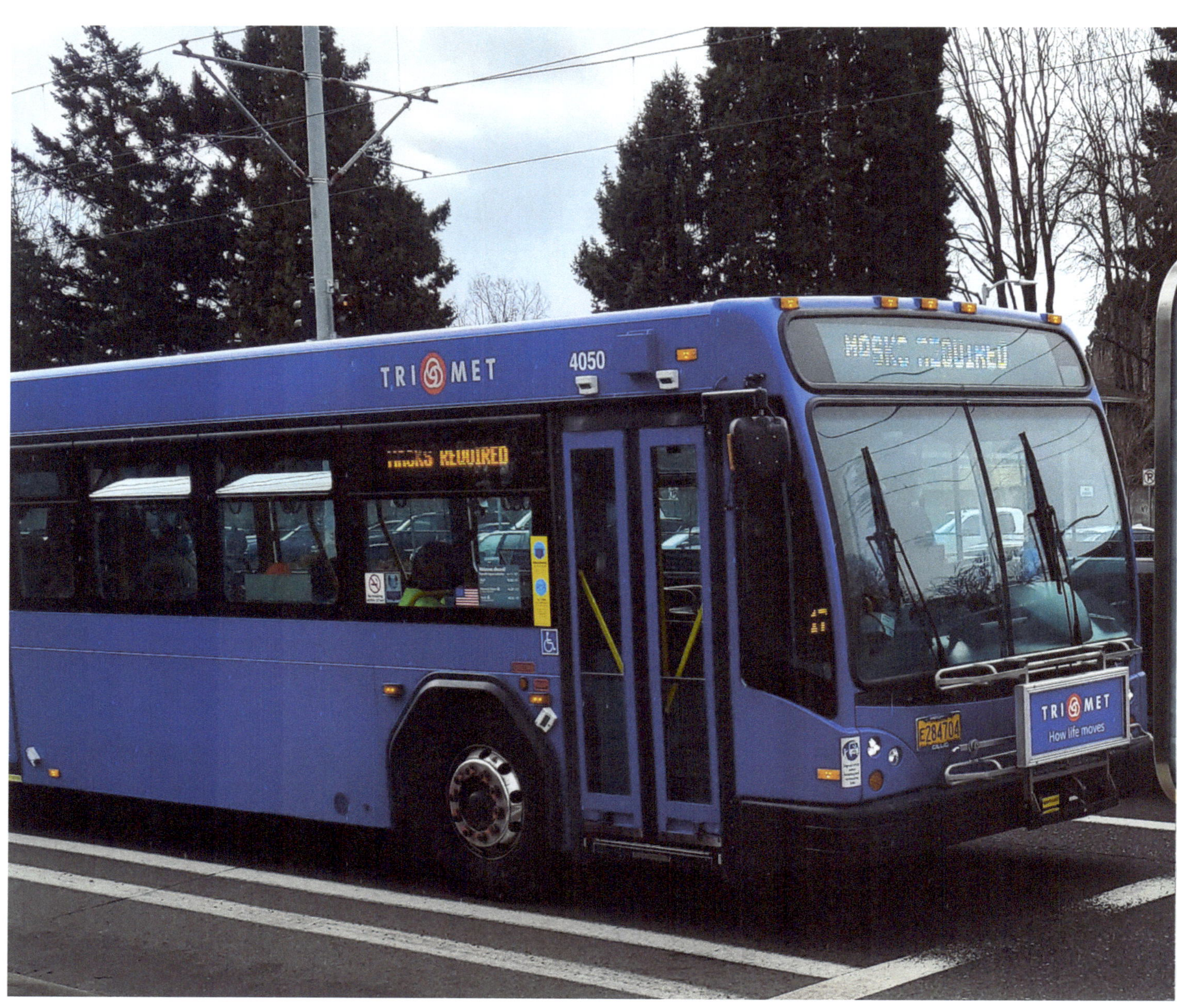
TRI MET
4050
TRI MET
How life moves
E284704

THE ACCIDENT APPEALS COMMITTEE

"Driver #2 sped through the red light at the intersection and slammed into my bus, causing damage to both vehicles, injuries to me and some of my passengers and to driver #2 and his one passenger. I was able to get access to the police records and found out that driver #2 was driving with expired license plates and had a history of drug abuse," stated bus operator C.M. in her case before the bus company's Accident Appeals Committee. The Accident Appeals Committee was composed of a chairperson, 2 training supervisors, 2 veteran bus operators and a union representative. The training supervisors and bus operators could vote on any cases before them, and the chairperson had the power to break a tie. The union rep was there to make sure everything was done fairly. The bus company held its bus operators to a high standard, training them to constantly scan ahead, left, right and behind to proactively anticipate the actions of everyone else on the road, while giving their passengers a smooth and safe ride. An operator could be charged with a P.A. (Preventable Accident) if it was determined the operator did not follow their training to do everything possible to prevent the accident. Four Preventable Accidents in a two-year period or one serious totally Preventable Accident resulting in loss of life (fortunately there was only one such P.A. in the bus company's long history) could result in the bus operator losing his or her job.

The Accident Appeals committee members together had a total of almost 150 years of experience in transportation. All were, or had been bus operators themselves, so they all knew the pressures involved in navigating a 40-foot bus full of passengers through busy city streets. One spring morning the Accident Appeals Committee, all dressed in street clothes, met in a typically bland meeting room with a full day of reports, videos, and operators' testimonies ahead of them. One of the day's first cases was that of operator C.M., a middle-aged woman who walked in the room in her bus driver's uniform and a neck brace. She was wearing sensible glasses and sturdy black shoes and had medium-length grey- brown hair. She was known to some of the other bus drivers and to some of her passengers as someone who didn't take any shit from anyone. She'd been doing the bus driver thing for quite a while, and let everyone know it. None of that mattered to the committee, who were not there to judge her as a person, but to judge her case on the merits.

S.F., the committee chairperson, graciously welcomed bus operator C.M. to her appeal session and introduced her to the committee members. S.F. was a knowledgeable red-haired, light-complexioned man who had worked as a long-haul trucker, a bus tour driver and a city bus operator. He had also run his own charter bus service, driving pro and college sports teams and touring musicians and entertainers to their games and gigs. The committee included bus operator R.L., who had started driving for the bus company in his twenties and now was nearing retirement 40 years later; bus operator S.C., a lifelong musician and artist who had been with the bus company for 18 years after 4 years of delivering mail for the U.S. Postal Service; trainer M.N., a solid no-nonsense yet big-hearted woman who made the education of bus operators her special mission; and trainer A.D., a tall, striking woman in her thirties who had quickly risen up the ranks in the company using her ability to soak up detailed information like a sponge.

The chairperson began the proceedings by reading C.M.'s Accident Report out loud, showing videos of the incident on a screen on the wall, then giving C.M. the floor. The committee was all eyes and ears.

C.M. maintained that as her bus (vehicle #1) was crossing a busy intersection, a late model Ford pick-up truck (vehicle #2) ran a red light and barreled into her bus, causing serious damage to both vehicles and injuries to drivers and passengers. She was adamant in placing blame on the driver of vehicle #2. She referred to the pick-up driver's history of drug abuse and his expired license plates, saying that such a person needed to be kept off the road.

The committee asked, "What were your actions before you approached the intersection? Did you scan in all directions? When did you first see the pick-up truck? What did you do after the accident?"

C.M. answered that she had done everything that she had been trained to do, and urged the committee to rule it a Non-Preventable Accident. S.F. thanked C.M. for coming in, excused her from the meeting, and let her know she could expect a ruling in her company mail within a week.

Now it was time for the committee to go over everything with a fine-toothed comb, talk about it, and then vote.

The committee watched the video over and over again. They had the technical capability to track the speed of the bus as it entered the intersection and to see other vehicles approaching in all directions. S.C. noticed something and asked to S.F. to slow down the video and stop it a certain point before the bus entered the intersection. They all could see, at the top of the screen, that the traffic light was already red when the bus barreled through the intersection. It was bus operator C.M., not the driver of vehicle #2, who ran the red light. The vote was unanimous: Preventable Accident (P.A.).

Bus operator C.M. let everyone know she was none too pleased about the Accident Appeals Committee ruling and the stain it put on her record.

Three weeks later trainer M.N. was in the bus yard walking to her office. A bus nearly ran her down and she could swear it was deliberate. She looked inside the bus and saw bus operator C.M.

* # *

MINIATURE PLANET

I saw a miniature planet slowly spinning around,
with miniature sights and miniature sounds
and miniature cities and miniature towns and miniature people
with miniature brains
and miniature cars and miniature trains and miniature houses
and miniature planes
and miniature clouds with miniature rain and miniature rivers
and a miniature sea
and a miniature forest with miniature trees
I saw a miniature planet slowly spinning around,
with miniature sights and miniature sounds
and miniature cities and miniature towns and miniature people
with miniature lives
in miniature scenes with miniature thoughts and miniature dreams
and so, I sing this song with my miniature guitar, and here we are

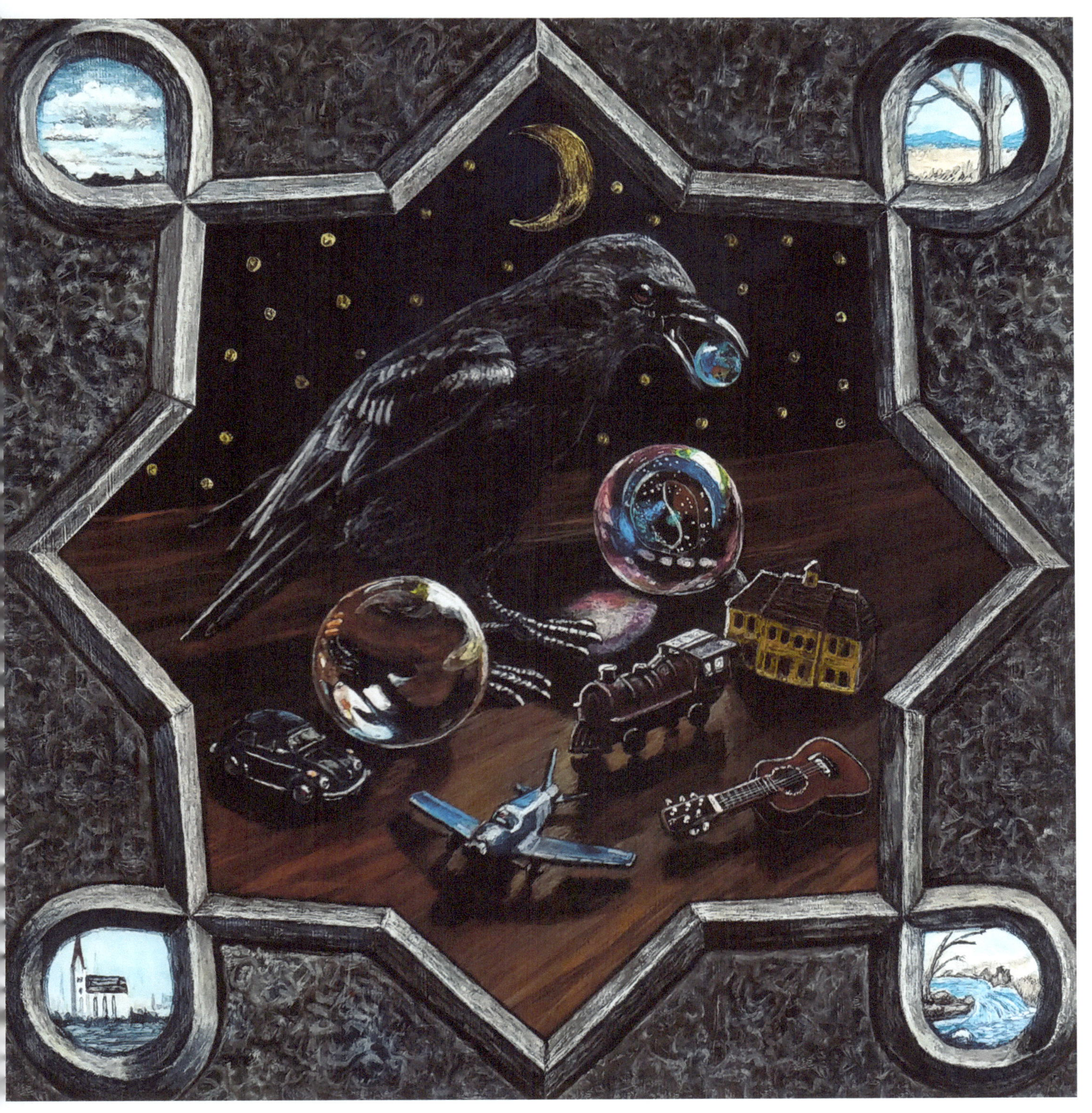

Christopher Shotola-Hardt
Illustration No.22: Crow Creates a Miniature Planet
acrylic on Masonite
12" x 12"

MARS MUSIC FESTIVAL

It was his custom to travel to and perform at a few music festivals every year. He found it easy to get to and from each festival but there were a few exceptions, like when he left a day early from Oregon to drive to a California winter festival over a mountain pass, only to drive into a winter storm, find the pass closed due to monster snow drifts and then detour down to the coast to find the coast road closed due to massive mud slides, or when he had to talk airline personnel at the Barcelona El-Prat Airport into letting him bring his custom acoustic guitar into the airplane passenger cabin when flying home from a festival in Spain, or when all physical festivals were cancelled during the Great Pandemic and he could only perform virtually at virtual festivals. But when he was invited to perform on Mars at the Mars Music Festival, well, that opened a whole new bag of travel challenges.

He made preparations for a 7-month, 200-million-mile journey to Mars, a yearlong stay there, and a long trip back home. There was a lot to do: pack all his instruments, gear, clothes, books and such, make arrangements to be away from home for more than 2 years, and prepare physically, mentally and emotionally for the experience. When the time came for take-off, he felt he was ready as he would ever be.

The take-off was a flaming success, and the spaceship left the earth's atmosphere without incident. Once in space, the ship was bombarded and battered by high-energy particles coming from solar flares but was not damaged, and the rest of the flight was relatively peaceful. The spaceship was occupied by a crew, several musicians and bands, and fifty music fans. Five other spaceships with similar human cargo left Earth before and after his ship to join 500 human permanent Martian residents at the music festival.

His spaceship had a safe landing after the 7-month journey in space. The Mars landscape reminded him of a few places he had been to in his earthly travels, like the Mohave Desert in California, the Sonoran Desert in Arizona, or the Lava Beds in Oregon, but on a whole different scale. A colorful, durable tent covered the festival grounds, sitting over the Mars terrain like a circus tent on Earth from centuries past. The Mars Music Festival was set up like some of the Earth festivals, with 2 alternating stages facing each other across a field filled with an audience of people sitting, standing, listening and dancing to the music. A hospitality tent for the performers and festival staff featured fresh food grown in artificially-lighted indoor Martian gardens. Red wine produced on Mars was available to everyone attending the festival. A buzz of anticipation could be felt through the crowd.

He performed his Martian Music Festival set, which was beamed across the universe. He looked forward to disappearing into the crowd and listening to the rest of the acts, something that he always enjoyed doing at festivals.

The alien band that followed him was totally unexpected, surprising everyone. Who were they? How did they get there? No one had ever seen or heard anything like it. They were out of this world.

* # *

ABOUT THE AUTHOR

3 Hand Stephen, a.k.a. Stephen Cohen, is a writer, a performing, recording, and visual artist and a singer/songwriter who has performed in concerts and at festivals across the United States and in Belgium and Spain. Stephen's first album, *The Tree People*, recorded in 1979, has been rediscovered in this century and reissued by record companies in Japan and Spain. His latest album release is *Where Do We Go?* Stephen's visual art has been featured at galleries, art fairs and festivals in Oregon and California. He lives in Lake Oswego, Oregon.

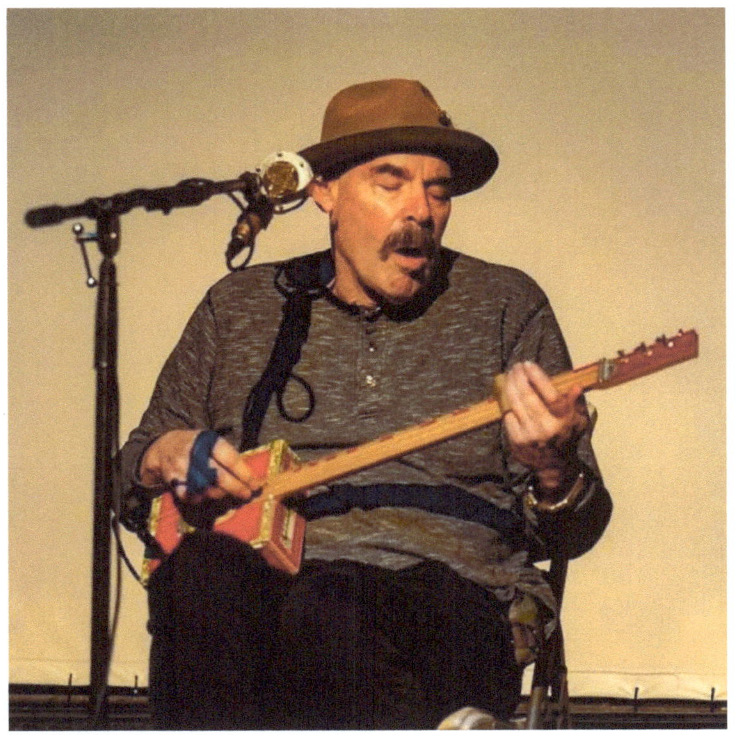

* # *

stories, poems, lyrics, illustrations, and sculptures
by Stephen Cohen, a.k.a. 3 Hand Stephen
www.3handstephen.com

Illustration No.22: Crow Creates a Miniature Planet
by Christopher Shotola-Hardt (p. 31)

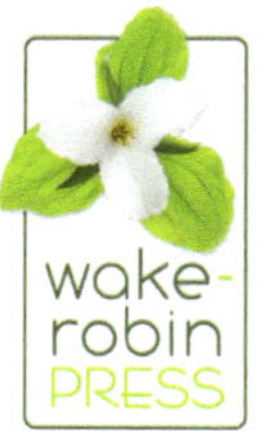
wake-
robin
PRESS

www.ingramcontent.com/pod-product-compliance
Lightning Source LLC
LaVergne TN
LVHW071633100826
845154LV00008BA/143
* 9 7 8 1 9 4 6 9 7 0 1 0 7 *